T0085808

LOOK AT HER

LOOK AT HER

Vanessa Shields

Black Moss
Press
2016

FIRST EDITION

Library and Archives Canada Cataloguing in Publication

Shields, Vanessa, 1978-, author
Look at her / Vanessa Shields.
Poems.
ISBN 978-0-88753-565-9 (paperback)
I. Title.

PS8637.H515L66 2016   C811'.6   C2016-903761-4

Editing: Marty Gervais
Cover Design: Nick Shields
Book Design: Karen Veryle Monck

Previously published poems:

• A Mother of Two Eats Alone In Her Car (Again) - *VerseAfire,* The Ontario
Poetry Society
• Kitchen Dancing - *Mind Shadows: Canadian Anthology of Poetry,* The Ontario
Poetry Society
• Recurring Childhood Memory - *VerseAfire,* The Ontario Poetry Society

 Black Moss
Press

Published by Black Moss Press
2450 Byng Road, Windsor, ON N8W 3E8 Canada
www.blackmosspress.com

Black Moss books are distributed in Canada and the U.S. by Fitzhenry &
Whiteside. All orders should be directed there.

Black Moss Press acknowledges the support of the Canada Council for the Arts
and the Ontario Arts Council for its publishing program.

ONTARIO ARTS COUNCIL
CONSEIL DES ARTS DE L'ONTARIO

 Canada Council   Conseil des Arts
for the Arts   du Canada

PRINTED IN CANADA

I dedicate this book to all the women in my life – young, old, wise, silly, brave, terrified... to all the women who have come before me writing poetry, singing songs, screaming for help, and all the women who will follow writing poetry, singing songs, screaming for help. I know you. I hear you. I support you. I write for you and with you.

To my daughter Miller whose love remakes me into the best woman I can be. I see you. I love you. Unconditionally. Thank you for loving me.

To my mother... there is always love.

CONTENTS

BODY

MOTHERHOOD

FAMILY

POWER

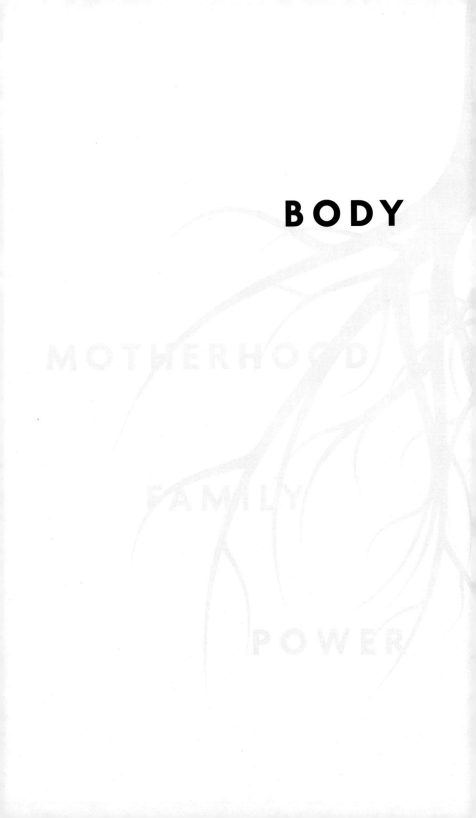

BODY

LOOK AT ME

if you looked at me like you wanted to be looked at
would that change how you looked at me?
would you see me differently?
if you wanted to?
where does your story end and mine begin?
when does your skin feel different than mine?
how many words are dancing in your blood?
how many vampires will we fight?
how does my clit rise differently than yours?
rise up!
aren't we supposed to rise up?
or are we to be still?
to hold the quiet in the braids of our hair
in the blood of our births
still be who we aren't sure how to be?

or are you sure?
certain like pain

that's how you want to look at me?

IT HAS HAPPENED

diane warren & lady ga-ga said
until it happens to you
   you don't know how it feels

  until it happens to you

on the floor in the dark
blanket under my shoulder
he planks against my back
pushes into my skin
i don't breathe
his arm comes around
i don't breathe
i millimeter forward
he falls back
this is war

  until it happens to you

crowded gym
music punches the walls
i dance
they circle me
push & rub & grab & laugh & rub

she writes
she plays piano
i listen

  did you tell anyone?

sort of i'm telling you now

IF HASHTAG WAS
AN HONOUR SYSTEM

Maybe if we didn't have to use words
Didn't have to say it out loud
Maybe if we could look you in the eye
And reach out our shaking hand
Maybe if you held us as we fell to the ground
Our legs weak from being forced open
Our wombs crying from being ravaged
Maybe we would tell you

Our souls have left our bodies
Detached

Maybe if a hashtag was an honour system
Maybe if a tweet was a prison sentence
Maybe if a music video was a magnet
To catch the ones who rape
One in every five

Our souls could flutter down and
Reattach

MY EYELASHES HAVE OPINIONS

I must get bigger
Don't be afraid to have an opinion

My eyelashes have opinions
The fingernails I bite off
Slather in spit
Toss out the car window
My body litter has opinions

Don't be afraid
To say it like the sun
The sun knows its heat

Be   the   sun

A LETTER OF REQUEST

Look, I'm not so bold as to assume that I'm the first to ever
write to you. I'm not so naïve as to believe you'd actually listen
and do what I ask it's just, I really want to love you and bring
you hours of pulsating pleasure and stop jamming cotton up
you when you decide to bleed.
I do love you, vagina. I do.
But I miss your elasticity.
I miss your pre-children, red-heated horny abundance and the
way we used to be best friends.
Will we ever be best friends again?

MY VAGINA IS NOT A HAYSTACK

My vagina is not a haystack
Yet I can feel a needle in her centre

For the rest of the day
I pee sideways

My button* tucked too much to
One side as if afraid to straighten

Settle into the safety and warmth of pink petals
A flower home heated and moist

I open and close my legs
To shift and move the folds

My vagina is not a haystack
Yet the needle is still there

Pricking the tip
Reminding me to love her

*where button = clitoris

DOING KEGELS AT STARBUCKS

I concentrate

Squeeze my vagina muscles
1-2-3-4-5
Look at the girls chattering at the table across from me
6-7-8-9-10
Check out how gorgeously hard & round that young girl's
Ass is in black tights
She dunks her tea bag in & out in & out of the hot water in
The paper cup
17-18-19-20-21

Damnit
This is more difficult than I thought
Don't smile
Don't laugh
29-30-31-32-33
I can only do five at a time
Look around
Holiday music pings my eardrums
37-38-39-40
No one knows
Take a deep breath
Get to 50

The girl behind the counter says,
"Please don't tell me how skinny I am!"
More black tights more hard asses
45-46-47-48-49-50

Find a piece of paper
Write a poem
Let the pen ink osmosis
The sound of youth –
Plough it into my vagina

The milk in my tea curdles at me
Looks like the cellulite on my thighs
I should know not to put milk in fruit tea
Next time   75 kegels
No milk in the tea

DON'T LOOK DOWN

My stomach is doing that thing it does
The waistband snuggles into the second and third roll
So when I look down I see a clothed PacMan
Or an ass with a really long crack
And I throw hate at it
Poke it with my fingers in disbelief
Stare at it like it's not really mine
Reach for a dull knife to cut it off in two big fat chunks
Throw it on the barbeque
Burn it

WHEN SHE SHOWED ME PORN ON HER CELL PHONE

She pulled out her phone
Tapped swiped and
Suddenly I saw porn
I felt the skin on my cheeks pulse with heat
She noticed and laughed at me
You? Embarrassed by porn?

She was shocked to hear I don't watch porn
Asked me why
I couldn't answer couldn't
Concentrate because I was watching the
Woman's face all scrunched and angry
Her neck twisted up as she looked back
At the man whose face I couldn't see
Plowing into her from behind
I didn't know what hole he was penetrating

Look at her face I said
How is she enjoying this?
That's why I can't watch porn
She said
Wait, you're looking at the woman?

Then her finger was back on the screen
A manicured nail pointing to the man's
Ass as it flexed and released
Look here, look at what the man's doing
That's what they do to us so that's where I look

So I looked but my eyes shifted back to the woman
She may as well have been looking up at me
Cursing me for watching her get banged by

A man whose face only she could see

I went back to the man
More flex and release
And flex and release
Then I sighed
Looked away

Nope, just doesn't do it for me I tell her
But thank you

DOGGY STYLE

In my mind I wasn't a dog

It was with the man I'd eventually
Marry that I rolled onto my knees
Arched my back and let him do it

Before then it was missionary
Maybe me on top perhaps a stint
On the side but never did I ruff it

Until he put those baby blues
On me and I felt a surge of
Woman that only he had
Jolted alive – Give a dog a bone

INCLUDING BUT NOT LIMITED TO

I want to gift you my body on special occasions
Including but not limited to:

> Birthdays
> Anniversaries
> Date nights (especially sleepover, mini-trips)
> Funerals (for grieving purposes)
> Weddings (other people's)
> Christmas work parties
> Thanksgiving
> Christmas Eve
> New Year's Eve

I will only say no on special occasions for the following reasons
Including but not limited to:

> Menstruation (at least the first few days)
> Exhaustion (from mothering, cleaning, cooking, etc.)
> Illness (flu, ulcerative colitis flare up, surgery, headache)
> Birth (give me at least 8 weeks)

BIRTHDAY SEX

I lean against the wall
Prop them up with wire
Bustier red lace spilling over
My stretch-marked mom belly
Feminine frills graze my
Rain-storm thighs
Black garter bow-ties
Hold up fishnet stockings
Slipped into red stilettos

I stand at the wall
Outside the bathroom
Waiting for you to notice me
Transformed
Tightly stuffed into
Your birthday gift wrapping

It's football on tv
But your eyes find my
Touchdown and your
Finger finds the remote
And the main event
Is me

I sing you happy birthday
As I strut to the bed
Crawl over you
Straddle your lengthening
Centre and we...

After, we both wonder
Out loud
Out of breath
Why every day isn't your birthday

WHEN YELLING AT MY KIDS WHILE BIKE RIDING COULD BE SEXUAL IF I CHANGED MY VOICE AND SAID THE WORDS TO MY HUSBAND WHILE WE WERE MAKING LOVE

Wait!
Wait!
Slow down
It's not safe!
Look where you're going!
I'm here
I'm here
Slow down!
It's not a race!
Don't get so close!
Turn right here
Slowly
Good job!
Okay, you can speed up a bit but stay close to me
Be careful!
You have to listen to me!
Turn here!
Now wait for me
I'm coming!
I'm coming!

NEW BRA

Give me nipples
>I like the raise of a chilled nipple
>Pushing through red lace
>A silent hello to a cold breeze or shifty eyes
>Proof of existence under a cotton shirt
>Business or pleasure the nipple lives
>There are bras for nipple motivation but the lift is less

Give me lift
>Like a smooth bum four inches from my double chin
>The padded bra takes the ladies up in thick cups
>Gently pushes together plump sacs of historied life
>Otherwise spread apart like droopy drunken noses
>A noticeable lift gravity defied stomach shrunken
>With the clip of the back straps smooth and adjustable

Nipples or lift?
I like a lengthy cleavage
But I like a hard nipple too
I can't have both in a bra

A MOTHER OF TWO EATS ALONE IN HER CAR (AGAIN)

I've taken to eating in the car
alone
again

okay (sigh)
I'm not totally
alone

there's NPR
talks of books movies politics spirituality
feeding me feeding me

there's Beyonce and grindin' up on that wood drunk in love and
rich people don't get hangovers they make music instead

this is our table to dine together
a lap a cup holder
a volume button
an on/off switch

I admit this is a problem
eating alone in my car

it's a building up of the foundation that is my stomach
so when I sit and feel the rolls one atop the other
I am reminded of the times I sat alone in my car
feeding my exhaustion
feeding my need for isolation
throwing out my guilt with the fast food garbage
so no one knows

IN THE SHOWER

Your skin smells like French fries and pasta
I hold your scent in my nose
Make a restaurant of you in my mouth
Remind myself that all this skin and scent
Is mine to love to inhale to hold
Beyond death do us part

There are pieces that don't align
Ribs that won't rub as I embrace you
The shapes of us growing sagging shifting
With life and age and time
But it doesn't matter

There are no borders between our souls
There is no war between our heartbeats
We wash each other before we make love
Laugh at the sound of the water squishing
Splashing between us

Your skin smells like French fries and pasta
Even after

LOOKING ON-LINE
FOR A DRESS TO WEAR
TO MY BEST FRIEND'S WEDDING

Polyester satin cotton chartreuse beige blues
Hues dots flowers pleats strapless
B-cup V-neck high-waist no waste what a waste
Pin stripe crinoline criss-cross strappy sleeveless
A-line B-line flat-line binge-eater hot throat
Unreal very real problems with the bodies

And the sign read 'Get Rid Of That Mom Belly'
Bright green letters burning tears in my eyes
Anger slow-cooking under my ribs
Rising like the lipo-sucked fat sludge sucking
Confidence from an already self-conscious woman

Get Rid of That Mom Belly?
That's the deleting
Of a history no skinny jean can steal
Curse the one who made that sign
Curse the one who made that face at the
Gorgeous fat dimples and the smooth purple
Stretch marks of new life being made in my
Mom belly in my miracle womb in my lovin' oven
This   is life   in lived-in skin

I'm the woman in the mirror I need to be strong

I'm all Julia Roberts laugh and
Meryl Streep deep and Maya Angelou
Soul-searching love-oozing
Neruda rooting Judy Blume blooming
Poetry with words so fat and jiggly
I cannot be contained

I TURNED TO PAPER

cut me open
pull out my liver
pull out my kidneys
excuse the paper
ignore the words, please

        or don't

the scales were always off, see?
paper soaked with blood and water
gets heavy so heavy in a bag of skin

        that's what you'll find

rambunctious words
splayed on crumpled paper
twisted over arteries
molded into muscles

        I wrote so much in this life

it was the words that punctured
the lymphnodes and slowed the t-cells
the words that choked the cancer
and strangled the esophagus

        that's why I got so quiet

all those day closings and
night openings when everything
was a fitzgerald description
a hemmingway plot line
a neruda romance with
rilke spit holding me together

I turned to paper

in the hospital bed while the nurses
complained and the doctors schemed
I watched in awe as black letters
pushed to my skin surface and
showed me the story of my life

read me now

I CLOSE MY EYES

You are Tom Cruise fingers
You are Adam Levine tongue
You are Channing Tatum stomach
You are Ryan Reynolds lips

Heated darkness
Hushed sounds
Lips and spit and skin
Fantasy is pleasure
And that's okay

NOT THE ONLY WOMAN

I am
standing
still
afraid to be the woman I am

every day I weaken
minuscule cracks in my body bag of skin widen
my son says I wear a scarf to cover my double chin

these chins
the chins of my dead grandfather
the chins of my wise aunt
the chins of my 86-year-old grandmother who knits with
knotted knuckles clanking metal needles she can still thread a
needle faster than I a seamstress life she holds creativity in the
rolls of her finger bones & she always tells me
I'm beautiful the most beautiful

I want to believe her but the demons are strong

it takes courage to receive a compliment to spread it over
my body to hold it in my skin on my chins in my cellulite
between the rolls my belly makes when I sit *I know I know*

I can do it
I can love the body I'm in
I can treat it like the vessel it is
I can hold it like it's not *me*
hold it like a blanket I'm quilting
       over time & space
       threading my life needle with courage

I am a woman
my body is my story
my chins are my ancestors
my wrinkles are my choices
my smile is pulled from the past

I am not the only woman who is afraid

can you hold me then?
hold me in your fear?
lather me in your light
I can see your beauty so easily like you can see mine
let's wear each other until we're strong enough to love our selves

MOTHERHOOD

THE RUBY BETWEEN MY THIGHS

I want to tell you I'm a mother
And you not look at me like I'm a child
With dirty innocence on my skin
Stretch-marked   bleeding
The love of this planet spinning on the tip of my tired nipple

You suck too hard   too often   too much
I need to replenish
I need to sleep
To wash you off my lips
Scrub your seed from my cheek
Laugh in your ear and   scratch   your back your DNA is
Under my nails

I want to tell you I'm a mother
And you bow down
Grow your beard and fill your wine jugs
Pour and caress
My weary feet with your hairy chin
Cook me a meal that makes you a slave then clean it all up
Then   make me a coffee

I want to tell you I'm a mother
And you get up on a chair and clap   slap your palms raw
Over and over and over
Never stop screaming my praise yell till your
Vocal chords tear and
Your tongue turns purple push out a baby with the sheer
Will of your being

I want to tell you I'm a mother
And you respect me for being the whore
Who keeps humanity glimmering   dripping   from
The ruby between my thighs

I HAVE A DAUGHTER

I watch her playing with the dog in the yard
Her high-pitched voice knows only joy and gentle need

She is not afraid to come home

There is no man here who will hit her with his hands
There is no woman here who will hit her with her words

I have a daughter

I watch her playing with the dog in the yard
She is the movie I dreamed for myself each night
In my childhood beds

HEARTSTRINGS

I envision crashing my car into oncoming traffic during rush
hour on the expressway between Howard and Dougall. The
on-off ramps no one knows how to use. I rage but it's only a
flavour of rage sweeter than the others. I don't crash. I don't kill.

I hold my daughter in my arms. Watch her fall asleep. Safe.
Warm. In the darkness, I see a man attempting to molest her.
I feel a rage that is beautiful and peaceful in killing him with
my bare hands. I kill him. This rage is tangible. Acceptable.
I understand the blindness of protection. Mother's instinct.
Unconditional love.

Are these thoughts preparation for a potential fate that
destiny holds over me – her strings attached to my heart?
Are those the heartstrings you talk about? Not musical. Not
attached to an instrument. Unless the instrument is rage.
Waiting. Patient. Quiet. Necessary.

AFTER A PHONE CALL
WITH MY MOTHER

There is a mouth of rage in my belly
Opening opening swallowing me up

I keep my own mouth shut or tell her I'm sorry
In my rage there is a disconnect
A pulling away of my innards
From the house where my soul lives

She yells when she cries
Her anger a tornado hungry for damage
Sucking sucking my strength to believe her this time

Even when it's cancer and broken bones
That mouth of rage in my belly bares her teeth
Sticks out her slithery tongue and keeps me away from my self

What do I really think of her?
What do I really believe?
Diseases tell stories but
I manipulate them to make them my own
Beginnings   middles   ends
Everything a storyteller's nightmare

She fights her demises with tears and anger
Also   confidence and courageous grace
Gets dressed up gets her hair and make-up done
For chemo treatments
Pretty for poison it's romantic, really

I'm exhausted under her fragility
I don't understand myself
In the reflections of her
I'm afraid of my rage
It connects me to her

IF I LISTEN

I hear myself apologizing for not being home sooner
As if in my absence our world dims and only my light
Brings the right illumination

I hear myself lie because I can't find the truth
When the story keeps changing because I can't
Find the glue to hold the pages together

I hear myself tell everyone but you that
I'm afraid

I'm afraid of the past that keeps wrestling for
The championship trophy of my existence

But I don't want to be defined
I don't want to be labeled
Like the baggage I've already organized

I want to keep the past just over there
In the dull glory of my blind spot so I can see it if I turn my head
So I can grab something if I need it for clarification or to burn

I hear myself agreeing when I don't agree at all
And I don't   know   why

I hear myself whisper through the creases of my lips
You're a mother you're a mother
And I don't know what it means

Mostly... I'm afraid of what you think of me
Mostly... I'm afraid you'll figure out I'm barely here
What you see is a shiver of my storm

I hear *everything*
Even your love on my skin
I hear
It all scares me

It scares me to love you from here
Where I'm not sure how to breathe out the sounds
Begging forgiveness

When I wake you in the morning
By kissing your palm
That's me
Transferring me
To you

Why do I ask if it's okay to love you this way?
While your light   flickering   flickering
Skids off your lashes onto my shoulders
Weightless?

I hear myself unraveling
The moon at my neck like a vampire

GIVE ME ALONE

Give me a Monday afternoon
I'll give you a poem from a different part of my soul
Give me a Monday afternoon
I'll peel back my skin and reveal darkness and light

Give me a Monday afternoon
I won't care the second hand on the clock
Is the loudest sound in the house
Let the seconds float around me
Not even Time can unzip my codes

Give me a Monday afternoon
I'll pretend that I'm okay maybe even believe it
While I meditate

Give me a Monday afternoon
I'll unshrivel enough to get a good look at my aging reflection
In the white of the laptop screen

Give me a Monday afternoon
I won't talk I'll give my tongue a rest
My throat can sleep when it doesn't have to dream
I'll sleep better tonight

Give me alone
On a Monday afternoon
It will get harder and harder to write
Harder and harder to be the oven
When what I really need is to be the bread
Unleavened unsalted
Substantial pure

Enough to feed a people out of a desert

THE SOUNDS OF HER

I'm called to her day camp
She runs to me
I gather her warm body in my arms

Mom my stomach is upside down
My heart is in my knees
Her illness descriptions are precise

Later   at home she lies
On the dog-haired floor
Wearing only her brother's
Too-small underwear

Folds her legs in half
Opens them closes them
Asks   *can you hear that?*
Smiling as she listens to the sound of
Her self opening and closing

I laugh at her genius
At her ability to pay attention
To describe things in a way
That blows my poet mind

Mom she asks as I tuck her in *Am I a good artist?*
Oh yes I tell her placing my finger on her heart
You're a brilliant artist because you create from your heart
Art rhymes with heart she says
Is my art so good you want to throw up?

Yes   I tell her   Always yes

POEM FROM A DEAD MOTHER
TO HER NEWBORN DAUGHTER

Listen
Your skin will call out to me
I will answer with my lashes
Wishes blown from heaven to breathe
Dream life into your soul

Feel me in the chiseled round of your chin
See me in the green shards of your eyes
Touch me in the storied lines of your palms
Where you held onto me
My womb your life vessel

See me lift out of my body to free you
From the sorrow of seeing it broken
This heart was made to shatter for you
I've pressed the pieces into your soul
To give it strength
To give it weight
To give it wisdom

Know me in your darkest of darks, Daughter
I made you from the glistening of tears that
Mourned my ascension

Hold me
I am everything
Your soul is a patchwork of my essences
We are seamstresses of misunderstood Fate
But when you close your eyes, Daughter
Don't misunderstand

Hold me in the knowing

I THINK ABOUT THE MOTHERS

Later I'm alone
Outside in my front yard
Beneath the maple tree strong and free
Leaves turning yellows and oranges only nature can make
I rake and rake for hours
I rake and rake can't stop looking up at the leaves
The ones that haven't fallen
The ones that are still holding on
Flickering on a wind I know is there because
The leaves are showing me

I think about the mothers

My kids are eating popsicles and watching Sponge Bob
I want it that way
I'm thinking about the mother of the soldiers
The mother of the police officers
The mother of the man who pulled the first
Trigger in broad daylight
Under the same sky
Maple trees watching

I'm thinking about the shooter's morning
The soldier who was shot
Did he eat breakfast? Did he shave?
Did he kiss his kids goodbye?
I think about the last thing he said to his mother

I watch the steel fingers of the rake gather fallen leaves
I rake and pile rake and pile then I reach down and
Scoop the leaves use the rake like a third hand
I curse the leaves that don't go in the bag

I curse whatever's causing pain in my left knee and
I curse my sore back

Guilt rolls over me like a black denim tidal wave
I fall to my knees and cry cry in the leafy muddy
Mulch of my front lawn

This day is perfect for raking
Perfect for singing and dancing and
Feeling alive and grateful and safe

I hear a news story comparing Canada's news coverage to
The coverage by the United States and how we put them to
Shame shame shame
Shame on everyone
Shame on me
Shame on the blue sky and yellow leaves and a
Maple tree strong and free shame on
Answers that make me sick to my stomach
Answers that make me never want to leave my house
Answers I can't tell my kids

I think about how different we each are and
How the same we each are
How we haven't yet figured out how to be human
To live as humans
No countries
No religion
No war
No heaven
No hell
I think about these words as lyrics written by a man
He was shot too

I think about how the words
Attack terror fear
Plague our days as sure as the leaves will fall
Each autumn season as sure as they will grow back

I run inside
Take my kids in my arms
Tell them over and over again
I love you
I love you
I love you

For the rest of the night
My daughter sings Oh Canada
Over and over and over

TELL ME

Can you just tell me
Send me a sign
A letter from wherever you are
Find something that's like paper
Use your words

Tell me I'm a good mother

WHAT'S LEFT OF ME

Some days I'm so empty
I can fill three black holes with my floating soul
I am outside myself
Beside myself
My brain is an organ untraceable
Yet I can hear it laughing in a distance
Just beyond the reach of my ear

Some days I yearn for aloneness like a shadow its freedom or its
life
Maybe I'm more like a shadow than anything else
I'm here when the sun allows me to be
Beside you
Creeping up on you
Eagerly edging closer to you until
It looks like we become one
But really I just disappear

The ache in my chest doesn't come from my heart
It comes from whatever's beneath my feet
Whatever's at the tips of my hair
Whatever's making my skin crawl or swell or burn

My heart is strong
It's a force that keeps me
Holds me
Pulls me back when even the darkness can't find me

So what is left of me?

I hear my mother's voice in my head
Scraping and clawing with the fingernails of my youth
She wants so badly to hold on but my blood is boiling

I feel my sister's screams in my throat
Gasping and choking the broken mirrors of our youth
I want so badly to sweep the shards away

After we lie to each other's faces
After we talk behind each other's backs
After we ignore and judge and compare

What's left of me?

I am the woman who writes about it
Living in fear
In shame
In constant recoil and you can
Never ever tell
You can never
See how the stitches of my worries
Make scars that puff and pink
I pick them   I pick them
And make wishes like on blown eyelashes
Wishing the same things over and over again

The hope blows me over like an angry winter squall
I fall to my knees
My hands slam the ground
Tiny rocks in my palms

What's left of me?

We love like it's all that matters
We fuck like it's not a secret but a wet release
A language of lips and heat and sweat

And mostly
I can't believe you still want me
With my wild dreams and my flabby belly
You still want my hips lifted up
My back to be your blank canvas
When the come makes me blind
When the nightmares make me break
When the knowing of letting you go
Happens every minute
You're away... or here

What's left of me?
When the kids are safe and sleeping
When the puppy dreams of chasing leaves
When the clocks in the house are music not movement
And the night welcomes my words like they were lost and found

What's left is everything

YOUR WOMB REMAINS

There are no photos of you pregnant
With me swelling up your womb
There are no stories but for the one
You tell me on my birthdays
How your labour was smooth short
How I was skinny and long like a naked bird

I wish I could remember being
Wrapped in your skin
Swimming in your fluids
Connected for life

Was my birth the beginning of our slow death?
Quiet like moments when I dream you
Put your hand on your belly
Whisper promises and premonitions
Did you beg me not to leave you?

Your womb remains
In the tint of my skin
I think I hear you
Echoing
Skin itches

SON

The aboriginal elder said
He'd never seen a connection
Like this before

On that Sunday
Twenty-eight years later
No champagne to drink
Just pitocin
Epidural numbness
Vomit in a green kidney dish

Everyone rallied
10 hours 15 20
No showers
Same clothes
Bad food
Prayers and whispers and worries
And love

In the twenty-seventh hour
The doctor pulled you out
With forceps

Your father saw first
You were a boy
He told me and cut the cord
We cried but
When the nurse put you
On my chest
I felt your lifeblood
I looked into your
Wrinkles and kissed
Our future into your skin

Son
I dreamed you like the earth
Dreams greens blues rainbows
My womb bears the shape of our love

We were both born on a Sunday
Our stories connected forever
And the aboriginal elder
Smiles at the stars we've aligned

DON'T

Don't buy a calendar with cute
Puppy golden retrievers
Fluffy sweet staring at you as
You hump
Don't mark that calendar
With a giant black X
Each day you hump
Don't try and remember
What you ate for dinner
What underwear he pulled off
What position you were in when
He rammed deep into your folds
And came
Don't squeeze your eyes closed
Pull your knees to your chest
Hold the semen in your womb
Don't lie beside him and say
Do you think we just made a baby?

CANOE

In those days
Canoeing was essential
A thrice-yearly tradition
Lugging tired brain and bones
Into the thick veiny trails of Algonquin
I could carry a canoe on my shoulders
A food pack on my chest
A backpack on my back

I was born to portage
My skin smudged with dirt
My hair tangled with leaves

When the moose paused
In the rocky shallows of
The dark crystal waters
He looked at me and I understood

I sat centre that first trip
Then moved up to stern
My arms strengthening
With each paddle pass

The priest said it was time
Time for my own canoe
His puppet-thick hands
Gesturing toward the bow

Now a painted paddle
Hangs on the wall beside my bed
My brain and bones tired and crooked

I'm the moose at the rocky edge
Remnants of Algonquin stuck
In my teeth curdled under my skin

She tells me there's Metis in my blood
I can feel it trundle in my deep like a canoe
When it first slides into a perfect black lake

I was born to portage
I am in need of remembering

NO MONEY

I remember I was eating a Whopper with cheese and bacon
minus the onions I hate onions I remember crying so hard
I could barely chew and couldn't swallow at all my words
spilling out of my over-spitted mouth with chunks of mayo
and bread and beef I remember the deepness of my fear
beneath my belly in the bowels of my bowels I remember
shame painting my skin reds and a rage that only poverty
can create I remember no money I remember oceans of
hopeless drowning the light and darkness burning me like fire
I remember your face and the pile of mangled Whopper and
guilt for not forcing myself to finish eating it I remember your
eyes so blue like heaven's skies and the silence you held us in
I remember how love saved us

BIRTH STORY

I ate a massive gyro
Then lay on the sofa
Like a resting whale
While your father worked
And I waited

Bridget Jones smoking and sexing
Writing in her journal
Worrying about her weight
Just get pregnant
It's the best kinda fat

Then it's pee
But not pee
Waters be broken
Heart be racin'
Hubby be drivin' home

And we filled the hospital room
With shitloads of stuff
Birth plan
Journal
Music by Madonna
Family and friends
In the hallway outside our door
A party began for you

And we waited
I bounced on a giant ball
I took a shower
I ate a peanut butter banana sandwich
I burped garlic gyro peanut butter breath
Until the epidural

Then I puked it all out
Emptied but for you and

You   took   your   sweet   old   time

The pain was barely bearable

After with you warm on my breasts
The doctor stitched and stitched and stitched
My vagina was never the same
Nothing was

DROWNING

I watched the film The Hours
Read the book too

There's a character   a mother
She can't breathe

So she leaves
Her house
Her child

She's lying on a bed in a hotel room
She closes her eyes and water pours through the walls
Drowning her

I understand

Were you drowning too?

WOUNDED

My cunt is built like a wound that won't heal
Ani DiFranco, Out of Habit

I can't get her voice out of my forehead
Her words scar my veins like drug needle tracks and
Like a drug she gives me leave

My cunt is built like a wound that won't heal
I get power when I think it
I get power when she sings it
I feel power when I feel it swell and thicken

My wounds are words
I'm afraid to scream stop
Stick my hand on your face
Push it away
Mutilate your
Pleasure like you
Mutilate mine

Our cunts are built to live like wounds
Folded stories stretching lips bearing gifts
Of human life over and over and over again

My hood is mother
My cunt is wounded but
Still I dream and lead and teach
Still I fear and weep and fail

Like a drug she gives me leave
From the fear and I listen to her tracks
I'm high on her power
Her beautiful cunt that won't heal
Heals me
We are wounded and perfect

CRYERS & PEE-ERS

It's not just the double chins
The thick brick-shaped shoulders or
The protruding bellies no belt can hold in

It's not just the anxious guts
The power-full breasts or
The nose that says Roman descent

It's not just the wide nail beds
The poking-out foot bone or
The sweets-craving palette

It's all of these parts - and
The tears and the pee

We are generations of cryers and pee-ers
Weak bladders mixed with weak ducts
We cry at commercials and songs about love
We pee when we laugh or jump or run

Mothers and sisters
Aunts and cousins
Strong-bodied
Strong-willed
Strong-minded

Strong-hearted

MY NONNA STOPS ME IN THE KITCHEN

I'm bending down to pick up my daughter's sock.
My Nonna puts her crumpled hand on my shoulder.

You have a culo* like your father.
I put my hand on hers, turn and face her.

I do?
You do.

It sticks out like his did.
Like a bubble.
I turn my neck and look over at my bum.
It does stick out like a bubble.

You're funny like he was too.
He used to make us laugh so much.

Thanks Nonna.
I squeeze her hand.

Remember that my father spent
Time in this kitchen.

Maybe he bent down to pick up one of my socks.
Maybe my Nonna told him he had a bubble bum.

Maybe he shook it and made her laugh.

culo is bum in Italian.

FAMILY

MORNING RITUAL

in those quiet mornings
cramped in a small bathroom
I learned things that school didn't teach
that life could barely breathe

it was her nudity that I clung to
let my eyes blanket her slight curves
her firm breasts faint cellulite pocking
the skin beneath her buttocks

I would sit on the toilet
tired and waiting for
sleep to release me
and watch her

my mother
spreading cream on her
arms legs belly breasts
we didn't know that cancer would take one

my mother
a steady strong passionate fighter
upholding a morning ritual
I would find myself copying

my mother
taught me to embrace my nudity
keep my skin moist
build rituals rolled on early
mornings with the sun peeking
through the dusty blinds

hear the clinking of bracelets
hear the sounds of her readying herself
for another day of single motherhood
another day of anger-laden motivation
working for money that was never enough

and hear the spray of Alfred Sung
and know I'd never forget
my mother
naked
in the mornings of my youth

KITCHEN DANCING

our history is laced with delicate memories of full-bellied
laughs young hands grasped in old lambada music blaring
from the radio on the spaghetti-sauce spilled counter in the
kitchen after a three-hour six-course Italian meal steeped in
tradition and garlic the women take to the cooking room to
do dishes put leftover mashed potatoes and green beans and
pasta and chicken in old margarine containers with mis-
matched lids Nonna fills the sink with hot sudsy water her
hips swaying a waltz to the sexy latin beats always she waltzes
my aunt scoops me up in her long strong arms and spins me
around like I'm a table cloth in the washing machine when
she puts me down I'm deney terrio on dance fever all gyrating
and chest pumping but the best thread in this lacey memory
is when Nonno steps onto the linoleum dance floor without
words my Nonna brings her body and attention from the
dishes to my grandfather's arms and she fits better than his
best shirt the music is hot and spicy but their moves are serene
and buttery I know this is one of the few ways he tells her he
loves her to brave his person into the woman's territory take
his love in his arms and sweep her off her feet he'd never use
a broom in that kitchen not when he could be sweeping her
sweeping us into his quiet devotion

CELEBRATION FLOWERS

he came home with garden arms
one holding a bouquet of flowers
the other potted mini-roses
all in celebration of the completion
of the writing of my young adult novel
the body of work
heavier than all the bricks
messier than all the rooms in all
the houses it took to write it in

within days the water feeding the bouquet
turned blue from the dye-infused daisies
snuggled between baby's breath and Peruvian lilies
it made me marvel and at the same time drop
my head in shame at the things we do for colour
at the things we do to change nature
at the way we manipulate something beautiful

yet the water was a toxic blue that caught my eyes
each time I passed the vase plunked between the
dusty stereo and the fruit-fly quilted bananas looking
more like giraffe necks than sunshine rays

the mini-roses thrived among eraser shreds and
unfinished poetry on the dining room table sucking sun
through the greasy hand-printed sliding glass doors
leading to the tired backyard

AVOIDANCE

I vacuum to avoid doing laundry.
I change the bed sheets to avoid vacuuming.
I fold clothes to avoid doing dishes.
I do dishes to avoid putting the folded clothes away.
I visit family to avoid doing groceries.
I do groceries to avoid cleaning the house.
I text to avoid talking on the phone.
I talk on the phone to avoid visiting someone.
I send emails to avoid making a phone call.
I read a novel to avoid writing one.
I write in my journal to avoid writing poetry.
I write poetry to avoid telling the truth.
I tell a lie to avoid feeling scared.
I eat chocolate to avoid feeling sad.
I pretend to sleep to avoid having sex.
I have sex to avoid doing laundry.

RECURRING CHILDHOOD NIGHTMARE

1415 Ellis Street East
on the corner of Ellis and Moy

the dining room at the
red maple wood table
matching maple chairs
my mother's prized pieces

family meal over
stained tablecloth
laughter joy comfort
ransacked by three men in
black clothes black holes
where faces should be

guns up bullets fired
no time for screams
I'm hit in the arm
play dead

the men leave or disappear
I'm the only one alive
in the silent bloodbath

TOOO-WIT

brown owl said
"tooo-wit   toooo-wit   toooo-wooooooo"

in the church basement
i scavenged for cookies
crumbs on my uniform

brown owl held up two fingers
"toooo-wit   tooo-wit   tooo-woooo"

in the church basement
i listened for moans
where are the boys?
blue dresses of guides?
crumbs on my yellow & white tie

brown owl invited us over
"tooo-wit   toooooo-wit   tooooooo-woooooooo"

cramped apartment
daughter with mean eyes
where are the cookies?
no crumbs on my t-shirt

i don't remember the motto
"tooooo-wit   toooooooo-wit   toooo-woooooooooo"

ON THE CARPET

We stopped at Burger King before the big award ceremony
But there was nothing to celebrate in his company
Inside I was grateful he stopped to let us eat
Inside I was wishing he were a letter I could delete with my cursor

The ceremony was short and sweet
I got to read my poem called 'Spring'
Age twelve and already published
People smiled and applauded like

Morning dew landing on open petals
I didn't want to leave the stuffy library
In the car on the way home my body started to break
Heat slammed into my skin like bricks into windows

The soles of my feet tingled
My tongue itched
I made it up the stairs to the hallway
Before I fell on my face

Passed out from salmonella poisoning
When I awoke I turned my head and vomited
On the oatmeal-smooth-coloured carpet
Hot chewed up hamburger pouring out of my smiling lips

My mom's face red and terrified
My sister's screams bouncing off the walls
He was downstairs calling the ambulance
I sat up relieved relaxed regurgitated

So much attention on poor little me
It was all a grand poem
The barf on the carpet
A perfect title

THE FIRST TIME I WATCHED PORN

It pulsated out of an old television with bad reception
In the brown-carpeted brown-paneled living room
Of my sister's best friend
This was the pizza delivery pool cleaning days of porn with
Fake-breasted women with fuzzy perms and witch-nailed
Fingers holding cigarettes they never smoked but had red
Lipstick on the filters like bloody tattoos
This was bow-chicka-bow-bow music porn where men had
Red tans and hairy chests and giant penises that pointed
Straight out like chubby skin swords

Twelve-year-old girls and boys gathered on the floor and on
The couch friends from school too young to be watching too
Inquisitive to say no too scared to run away
Most of us never been kissed all virgins learning what horny
Felt like as our privates tightened or lengthened as we kept
Quiet and watched grateful no one looked at each other kept
Our eyes on the screen and our hands on our knees

Etched in the corridor of my virgin brain is a white woman
With brown hair waking in the night to the sound of her
Sister being screwed wood bed banging on the wall
Screams and moans of passion floating in the slit beneath
The closed bedroom door she bites her lip fully-lipsticked
Getting red on her teeth rolls her eyes back in ecstasy
Caresses her hard-nippled breast and reaches for her teddy
Bear wait her teddy bear?
And its head is in her bushy crotch and she's breathing hard
And she's rubbing its nose on her what is that thing?
And there's pee squirting everywhere why is she peeing?

She's yelling and writhing and there's more pee but it's not
Pee it's thicker and I close my eyes squeeze them tight pray
For this to end but someone's fast-forwarding
The VHS taped labeled MOM & DAD and I open my eyes
I'm sweating and scared and my crotch is throbbing and will
I pee my pants? And it's a puffy lippy hole with fingers
Jamming in and out one finger two fingers with no fake nails
But the other fingers still have long fake nails on them I
Guess that makes sense it would hurt to do that with fake
Nails on those fingers maybe she'd cut herself maybe it
Would fall off and get stuck in her vagina is that what a
Vagina looks like?
I will never look at mine
I will throw out all of my teddy bears

HIS SPIT

he licks my cheek
spit-slick tongue
he screams nigger pile
naked chest thump

i'm on my back

he licks my cheek
she's on top too
& her
then him
his spit

i can't breathe

69 (MY EYES)

a compromising position
face to penis
face to vagina
a position
eye can't compromise
eye promise eye can cum
but eye can't promise eye'll cum
when your nose is near my ass
your penis is in my mouth
eye promise not to compromise
my oral sex abilities
eye'd be compromising my self
my ability to cum
if you put me in this position
that would compromise
our relationship
eye love you
eye want to make you cum
eye can't tell you why
eye won't 69
eye promise on your penis
my vagina
that the reason
came at me when
eye was a child

my eyes were in
no position to understand
what they saw
my eyes
still see

AUGUST 26, 1996

We made love for the first time
Two horny teens on a futon bed
It wasn't a Judy Blume novel more like a
Danielle Steel first draft
He was gentle and excited

We did it before prom night but after our
One-year anniversary
We did it on the floor of my bedroom while
My mother slept in the room next door and
My sister slept in the room next to that

We were fooling around and I wanted to do it
I asked him if he had a condom
He said no then bolted up got dressed
Went to a store and got one
Came back got undressed and we were back at it

There was no blood
No cherry stains on my sheets
Wet pleasure a good orgasm

It didn't hurt

I THINK ABOUT YOU DYING

When you're gone
I can't sleep on your side of the bed
Instead I stroke the coldness of the sheet
Sniff the scent of your scalp that's seeped
Into the pillowcase
Put my hand over my heart to calm it down
It misses you so

I think about you dying
How awful is that?
The cold sheets make me do it
You're gone
Really gone and
With you my insides

I'd be hollow
Like cheap dollar store easter bunny chocolate
People will take a bite of me
Spit me out
Throw my remains in the trash

That'd be fine with me
Hollowed be my name
Be my body
A shell of a love so brilliant
It keeps a girl blind

SCALPEL LOVE

I love you like a scalpel loves skin
Love how you cut me open with your smile
How you hold my heart and guts
My emotions and my worries
In your hands and all of me seeps
Into your skin for safety

I love you more than the earth turns
Love how you turn me inside out
How you teach my voice to strengthen
My shoulders to steady and my ears to listen
In the white of the wisdom of your itchy goatee
You hold my courage like the earth its life

I love you like all the poets in the world
Got together to write love poetry
Sultry sonnets and astounding acrostics
Like all the ink in the world running
Through my veins burns for you
I love you like you're paper and
I'm the last poet
In the world to write on you

NAKED BODIES

I. mother
mornings in the bathroom
thongs on the door handle
two breasts
then one
scars
stretch marks
perfection

II. grandmother
upstairs in the big bathroom
nonna's house
sleepovers
one inch of water in the tub
scalding safety
water balloon breasts
bottom-heavy
strong tight round belly
clump of hemorrhoids

III. sister
shared bedrooms
changing clothes
after showers
similar shapes
earlier blooms
confident
skin unbreakable

IV. man
late night
bunk beds
penis dangle
black tuft of hair
fear
shock
curiosity
anger

V. lover
three
gentle touches
quiet beds
basement bedroom
holding
crying
moaning
climaxing

VI. self
anywhere
there
isn't
a mirror
saggy
playful
ashamed
building
confidence

LAST NAME

I got married and took his name
Leaving your behind in a disappointed sigh of childish anger
Now no one says it wrong
Or asks me if I'm French
Now it's – what comes first, the I or the E?
You're gone your body rotting in the ground
Six feet under and sinking

It wasn't an anti-feminist
I-belong-to-this-man-now plot

It was simply a little girl
Mad at her dad for not coming to her wedding
It was simply a little girl
Refusing to forgive and grow up

Simply
I'm sorry

TIME PASSED

How much time do you think should pass between your death
and when I can write poetry about you? It's been close to ten
years. Or maybe it's ten years this coming January. What does
it say about me that I don't know the date of your death? Or
the date of your birth for that matter? Maybe I don't deserve to
be a poet. To write poetry about you. What kind of daughter
doesn't know her father's... everything? If you were still alive
I'd ask you if you knew my birth date. And hope that you'd say
no. That you'd be honest about it. Then we both could let go of
the guilt of not knowing something so momentous. We could
go back to waiting for someone to tell us.

SELECTIVE SMELLING - DAD

Baked in rubber on sand-smeared cement.

Fresh-cut hand-dyed suede.

Soy-smothered sashimi tuna.

Yellow nicotine-thick fingertips.

Still-drying paint mixed with drywall dust.

Formaldehyde.

Shined-with-wax-and-sin church pews.

Open earth ripe with forgiveness.

CHILDHOOD DREAMS

They said you were a phenomenal baseball player. That the big leagues were calling your name. But you heard different voices and took to the green of the golf course. You loved the lawn. The life of it. The smell of it. The height and thickness of it. It is a meticulous plant to adore. But each blade meant a home run to you.

Later, after divorce and four kids, you bought a big house in the suburbs of Hamilton. You made a green on your front lawn. It was perfect. When I reached down to caress it, I felt your spirit in the dew hats.

MAJOR HOLIDAYS

You'd come and get us on major holidays like Christmas and Easter. When we had days off from school and mom was willing to share us. You grew up in LaSalle. Married my mom in Windsor. Divorced her there. Then you left and only came back to get us and whisk us away too.

Holidays were time rations in a cold war between you and mom. Did you want to come and get us? Did you call her to ask for us or did she call you to force it? Does it matter? My version of you was slathered in her anger. My stomach dislocated to somewhere in my calves. I was nervous to see you every time.

Minor holidays would have been better. You standing on the sidewalk as we skipped door-to-door on Halloween. Ice cream over warm pie on Valentine's Day. Maybe a stuffed red heart for us to put on our pillows. A green bowtie and a box of Pot of Gold for St. Patrick. Less pressure. Less time. Less confusion.

We were soldiers on a battlefield in a war that started when wars typically cease. I always wanted peace. Did you?

PHOTO OF YOU ON THE WALL
IN THE HALLWAY

A close up of your face
Full moon shape
Timid smile under
Black moustache
Shadow of a five o'clock shadow
Darkening your cheeks

My daughter stops
Head cocked to the side

Is that your dad?
Yes, that's him.
Is he dead?
Yup.
Oh.
His name was (is) Dale.
Dale?
Yeah.
That's a weird name.

She looks at me.
Takes my hand.

THE OTHER DADS

Even in your absence
You were better than them

I was never afraid of you like
I was afraid of them
The fear was different with you
Stuck in my chest
A fist around my heart
Pining for you to love me

The other dads were mean or translucent
A child needs kindness and colour
Thickness for both so she can learn how to trust

Even though I had trouble loving you
The want was always there

The other dads tried too hard or didn't try at all
You did your best that was more and less
But you never lied about what you could give
That was important even though it took me
Years to understand

I always understood
That the other dads
Were not you

THE FIGHT

Mom told me there was fistfight
Between you and another guy
     For   her

Clenched hands flew to ruddy cheekbones
As Roberta Flack belted out killing me softly
     She   hates

That song now
Makes me turn it off when it's
On the radio

I love it
In my bones

Thinking I'd be honoured
For you to fight for me

Instead
You kill me softly

POWER

LOOK AT HER

I look at her ears hear her sound round her lobe she strobes
I look at her eyes disguise lies her soul floors with dirt she skirts
I look at her chin sin layers she prays for change she maims
I look at her neck crane gain her trust bust burst she hurts
I look at her chest breasts heave cleave off she coughs
I look at her hips swish her lips lick tongue swipe ripe red
I look at her scars she scares the war is skin she pins she wins
I look at her woman hood good she glistens the gleam I listen

PEDESTALS

I can't see your eyes and the truths they tell when you're up
there and
I'm down here

The problem with pedestals is a problem of weight and
consequent hate or exhausted resentment you can't see my
eyes and the lies they tell when I'm down here and
you're up there

I have a problem with pedestals I build them and put you on them
carry you around like a foolish disciple

I do that I build you up I guess that makes you higher
I bury me down because
I forget my talent and that makes me less

And if I trip
It's you I catch
If I fall
It's you I comfort
Dust you off
Put you back up
Raise you high

IN MY NEXT LIFE

I will be a slut

A fun-loving
Safe-and-clean
Let's-party-and-fuck-all-night
Kinda slut

A by-choice slut because
Sex is fun and feels good
And makes me feel alive
And I want to feel alive with as many
People as I can
As often as I can

I won't be prejudiced or picky
Prudish or proud

I will French kiss until my lips
Bleed and bruise
Because the world needs more kissing

I will bring back foreplay
I will embrace pleasure toys
I will spin in the lace of expensive lingerie

I will be a jazz singer and
Wear long red gowns with no underwear
My vagina will be at my command
As I splay on piano tops in basement bars
Smoky with lust and lies

I will be a jazz singing slut

And I'll wear wigs to match my moods
And heels to match the colour of my soul
And I'll dance every day not on a stage or with a pole
But in the moments before I spread my legs
Over under up and down
Across the slut-studded universe

When my body gets tired
When my heart gets weak
When my vagina gets dry
Because it will
It will

I'll shut down my slut-dom
Look around and find my true love

He'll be old but I'll be old too
And when we hit the sack for afternoon naps
After we put our dentures on the bedside tables
I'll fuck him like the slut I was

I GO TO THE CARDS

I go to the cards because I can't find god
I need someone to peel the burn of my days
Off my shoulders   they slouch

I go to the cards because I believe
In magic and true love
It's how I pull poems out of air

I go to the cards because angels dance
On my forehead
My mind can be church
My congregation
The books on my shelves

I go to the cards because they're always there
Waiting for my grief
Offering it relief

I go to the cards because I'm lonely
A wish without an eyelash
A star without brilliance
A card without a deck
All of me in need of shuffling

VOID

It's not enough to run
Arms flailing
Hair matting
Skin sagging
Voice trailing in
A wake of frothy urges

I'm safe in the void
Rooting my sleepy feet
In quick sand

PARALLEL UNIVERSE

Grateful for the drive home

When the landscape shifts from

Bruised buildings oozing too much feeling

She turns onto smooth streets

Under lazy trees of yet another parallel

She understands that there is no *both*

At least not for her

As she nears what is precise

Lived in her chest opens then closes

She hopes the bruises don't show through

TAKING BACK MY SOUL

Was identifying myself as a writer even in those early teen
years a mistake? He knew it, didn't like it. And so the debate
about the meaning of Fitzgerald's blue light ensued and I got
a shitty mark on my essay. How do you know that's what he
meant? Did you ask him, I demanded. Back then I was so
literal. This fight was a meager storm. When poetry came
he was a roaring sea of nevers. Never write about writing.
Never use the word soul. Never question authority. Said loud
enough under his old-man breath of disdain for us to hear. For
me to hear. I heard it and it slayed me. For decades.

After my first broken heart I found my soul. Bleeding and
waiting. Tattooed on the skin over my right hip bone. African
tribal symbol for all to see. I took it back in the pain of
mending my heart. I took it back in the tear-driven poetry
that gathered all my pieces and stanza-ed them together again.

I thought of him then, the white-haired, soul-less English
teacher. I saw him in a crowded restaurant, a table away. I
went to him, all bravery and fear. He stood, still so tall, so
hovering. You were my best student, he told me. He still had
the white hair. The white moustache. The white soul.

All I could do was stare,
my teenage self a sloppy poem under his nose.

HAIR

for Dionne Brand's hair

The brain is an electric squish-ball
Billions of neurons blasting like
Bombs in universal wars
I want her nuclear fall-out to burn my skin
I want to eat her colours
Digest her DNA
Turn her sounds into words
Let them be sutures
Stitch me back together

I want to dive into Dionne's
Salty peppered afro
Feel the fire of her words
Taste the sugar of her love

I KNOW WHAT'S COMING
FOR EDITH

(After reading 'The Bell Jar' by Sylvia Plath)

Edith left a bad man's blood smeared across her cheek
So she could remember the moments of his atrocity
So she could see the violence of her encounter
She let it dry on her white skin until it crackled and itched
And flakes fell off into the wind she always threw stuff into
Her clothes her dreams

I know what's coming for Edith
I know what's coming for me
When I leave his words on my neck or
Her lies on my eyelids
Everything gets heavier
I get sleepier
Weaker and
Shrink so I
Can fall
Into the
Jar or
The

Darkness or the fantasy
Such living is not simple
But necessary?
I don't know
Purgatory is bland

SHE LEAVES THE RED

gorgeous red lips offer
       a movement
       a promise
       a portal
she wants to run her tongue
over its hills and valleys
the white teeth
lick them real

instead she weeps
       at her inability
       for fearlessness
she swallows herself again and again
watching time dangle choice chimes
like manna rain on eyelids

she leaves the red

IN THE DYING PART

The job of the woman is to engage the orgasm
Learn to lengthen its climax

Learn to evolve its innocent yearning
When she dares to ask

Is this love?

Somewhere inside the ripples and moans
The shudders of the aftermath is a thick confusion

The heroine sees the faults
In the walls hope can build

Is this love?

She understands that renovations
Are acceptable although

Time consuming and costly
She doesn't work for measurable wages

Is this love?

God she will be beautiful
White flour in her hair or maybe

It's dry wall dust or maybe it's cum
The heroin will see a new reflection

Is this love?

In the mirror it will get easier
To accept her crimson cheeks

Each time there will be less
Pain in the emptying

Less losing of herself
In the dying part of the orgasm

If this is love

IT'S WHAT SHE WANTED

the truth is
it's what she wanted
just not from him
not from his thick lips
his spit-shiny teeth
his sweat speckled forehead
it's beyond wrong but wrong's the wrong word
it didn't feel like she thought it would although
she never thought she would feel so alive
those words his words were gifts and
that was what she wanted so
she let him hear her laugh

THE GIRL STAIN

I'm the girl with bare shoulders burning in the 4 o'clock sun
With a neck glistening sultry sweat
Hair dark and tucked tightly behind soft-lobed ears

I'm the girl who pulls the words from your mouth into the
Sexy silence radiating between us

    If we never meet

The girl your tongue desires to taste
Every inch
Every darkness
Every fold
Your tongue is tied to a language only lust can speak

    If our bodies never connect

I'm the girl who breaks your eyes shatters those windows
So fiercely so fast your soul can't breathe

    I remain a stain

You'll spend the rest of your life
Searching for this unearthly feeling

    Unless

We meet and you stop and kiss me
Kiss me hard

WHERE DOES SHE PUT WHAT HE SAID?

Where does she put the lust in his eyes
  The dedication
  The attention
  The unrelenting fixation
On all the things she hides in her cloud

Where does she put the way his upper lip
  Curled over that scraggly white tooth
  Reaching for her eyes
  Those sounds stinging her burning ears
And shivering soul

His words were illegal according to unwritten law
  No one said those things
  No one dared cut the air
Steal her breath while she laughed like it was meaningless

      She put it away
      Sliced and stuffed into secrets
      Tucked it in a new wrinkle

PLAYBACK

He kept saying
No one's listening
That's important
Hold my hand
Say it
Say it
      Once

But this doesn't
Work for her
She's tightened skin
      Covered

He's a movie
She has to
      Let go

Press stop
Hold it
For playback

A STRAIGHT GIRL AND
A GAY GIRL TALK IN A CAR

i can tell by that heavy feeling my
bones get when they sink deeper into my body

it's past 3 in the morning
i can feel heat coming off her shoulder

i know she can feel heat coming off mine
i'm pretty sure you're gay she says

i throw my head back and laugh
i'm pretty sure i'm not

trust me, i've tried
i kissed a girl because i was attracted to her

she stares at my lips
and i wanted to feel something

anything - but i just... didn't
plus... i can't imagine going down on a girl

now it's her turn to throw her head back and laugh
you think that's all we do?

my cheeks flush
other places too

one night that's all it would take
i'd ravage you

i just... appreciate good people beautiful people
sometimes i think about kissing them

but when it comes to chicks
when i imagine, you know, fooling around

i can't get further than touching boobs
she turns to me and we're in that moment

that heavy horny daring terrifying moment
we teeter on the edge of every cliff and fence

she looks away first
damn

her words steal my breath
i think you would ravage me

she smiles
i look at her lips

the ring on my finger tightens

we get out of the car
our promises lingering

in the moisture
on the windows

THIS IS HOW WE FATTEN

Women meet for meals
Talk to feed our souls
Like salty tuna nigiri

Listen to hear our hearts
Like loose-leaf hot green tea

Liquid salve
Origami words

This is why our arms jiggle
This is why our hips sway

This the power of a full-bodied conversation
Made of stories

Chopped emotions
Sliced drama

Melted wisdom
Drizzled over sushi

Hotter than the greenest wasabi
This is how we fatten

Show me a plump female
I'll give you a best friend

A mother a daughter a lover
Who feasts on love and friendship

Succulent
Savoury

APOTHECARY

What would I mix
That would taste like
Anything that mattered
For the feast that is
Untraceable poison
Is the feast of the
Quiet woman
Dragging her opinions
Behind her

Though my apothecary
Shelves balance on rickety hope
I haven't started mixing
The potion that will
Make you listen

KNOWING

It's not the same
A room with all women in it
It's not the same as a room with men in it too

It's not the same
A room with all white people in it
It's not the same as a room with
stop you can't write this

Stick to your *knowing*

It's bullshit

She asked with such innocence
But what does it feel like to be black?

Everyone whooped and wahhhhhhed

No one answered

That was so long ago but it sticks to me like skin
It is my knowing

He slams poetry on a national stage fire burning behind him
Knees pumping arms flailing white people clapping
This is his Compton

This is my Compton
Knowing

You don't believe me

IN THE SILENCE

I can hear the skin-dusted air blowing through the vents &
the motor churn at the back of the old fridge
the wind whip-moans against our thinning windows &
the second hand on the clock matches my heart beat
> I think about who I am
> in this house
> loving these people
> in these ways

I read poetry by women I'll never meet
listen to music by men I'll never kiss
run my hand over cotton I didn't pick &
the defrosting meat on the stovetop melts its last shard of ice
> I think about who I might have been
> in another house
> loving other people
> in different ways

I feel the curve of a tear forming behind my esophagus
feel a wrinkle deepen in the skin around my eye
my bones tell me stories about rain
metaphors grow like hair off my skin

I am muddy water pounding over rocks
searching for land
I pray for stillness
so that when the silence comes
murdering over me
it will kill me proper
> I'll know who I am
> in this world
> loving everyone
> unconditionally &

I won't be afraid

ACKNOWLEDGEMENTS

Every writer writes: *This book couldn't have been written without the love and support of the following people.* That's because it's true. Although a writer's work may come out of collected solitary moments, what has to happen to reach and take advantage of these moments is the simple yet necessary love and support of family, friends, and the community in which a writer writes.

My writing community extends from the messy-ness of our family's dining room table to the tables of restaurants and bars, to the sides of roads, to the libraries and bookstores, to the classrooms in schools, and back to the dog-haired bed in which I sleep and dream. The city of Windsor is my writing community. Thank you to all the truly inspiring and incredible writers, chefs, business owners, and creative people who drive the robust and vibrant art collective that makes this city a place I choose to live, love and write in.

Thank you Marty (Gervais), my publisher, editor and dear friend. We are two poets meant to write and share together. Thank you for believing in my work, and my 'me'...and challenging me to 'change the world' with my poetry.

Thank you Nick, Jett and Miller, and Oscar my best and greatest works of art and love. Everything I do is for you. Thank you for keeping my heart bursting with passion. Babe, thank you for loving me so unconditionally.

I am grateful for the strong, kind, inspiring women and men who hold me in their lives as a best friend – on the page and off – Christopher, Karen, Penny-Anne, Janine, Cathy, Katie, Anne Marie, Linda, Danica... near and far, I don't fall because you hold me up.

Mom, Danah, Bisnonna – thank you for you.

With each poem I write, I am less afraid.

ABOUT THE AUTHOR

Shields has made her home, her family and her work
life flourish in Windsor, Ontario, Canada. Her passion for
writing was discovered at a very young age through the vein
of writing in a journal. Her first book, *Laughing Through
A Second Pregnancy – A Memoir,* was published by Black
Moss Press in 2011 to rave reviews. In April 2013, Shields
edited a poetry anthology entitled, *Whisky Sour City* (Black
Moss Press). *I Am That Woman,* her first book of poetry, was
published in January 2014, also by Black Moss Press. For
all things Vanessa, please visit www.vanessashields.com. She
looks forward to your visits!